WASHINGTON

Sarah Tieck

Big Buddy BOOKS
Explore the United States

VISIT US AT

www.abdopublishing.com

Published by ABDO Publishing Company, PO Box 398166, Minneapolis, MN 55439.

Copyright © 2013 by Abdo Consulting Group, Inc. International copyrights reserved in all countries. No part of this book may be reproduced in any form without written permission from the publisher. Big Buddy Books™ is a trademark and logo of ABDO Publishing Company.

Printed in the United States of America, North Mankato, Minnesota.
052012
092012

 PRINTED ON RECYCLED PAPER

Coordinating Series Editor: Rochelle Baltzer
Contributing Editors: Megan M. Gunderson, Marcia Zappa
Graphic Design: Adam Craven
Cover Photograph: *Shutterstock*: Rigucci.
Interior Photographs/Illustrations: *Alamy*: John Glover (p. 30), North Wind Picture Archives (p. 13); *Getty Images*: Keystone (p. 23), PAUL J. RICHARDS/AFP (p. 25); *Glow Images*: Wolfgang Kaehler (p. 11), Aaron Mccoy (p. 26), George Ostertag (p. 30); *iStockphoto*: ©iStockphoto.com/catscandotcom (p. 11), ©iStockphoto.com/ Darinburt (p. 19), ©iStockphoto.com/JuniperCreek (p. 27), ©iStockphoto.com/michieldb (p. 26), ©iStockphoto. com/Veni (p. 9); *Shutterstock*: 2009fotofriends (p. 29), Steve Bower (p. 21), Philip Lange (p. 30), L.L.Masseth (p. 27), Caitlin Mirra (p. 9), Al Mueller (p. 30), neelsky (p. 5), Bill Perry (p. 17), tusharkoley (p. 27).

All population figures taken from the 2010 US census.

Library of Congress Cataloging-in-Publication Data

Tieck, Sarah, 1976-
  Washington / Sarah Tieck.
    p. cm. -- (Explore the United States)
  ISBN 978-1-61783-386-1
  1. Washington (State)--Juvenile literature. I. Title.
  F891.3.T49 2013
  979.7--dc23
                                2012017506

WASHINGTON

Contents

ONE NATION

The United States is a **diverse** country. It has farmland, cities, coasts, and mountains. Its people come from many different backgrounds. And, its history covers more than 200 years.

Today the country includes 50 states. Washington is one of these states. Let's learn more about Washington and its story!

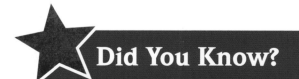

Did You Know?

Washington became a state on November 11, 1889. It was the forty-second state to join the nation.

4

Washington's highest point is Mount Rainier. This
famous mountain is 14,410 feet (4,392 m) tall.

WASHINGTON UP CLOSE

The United States has four main **regions**. Washington is in the West.

Washington has two states on its borders. Idaho is east and Oregon is south. The country of Canada is north. And, the Pacific Ocean is west.

Washington has a total area of 68,095 square miles (176,365 sq km). About 6.7 million people live there.

Did You Know?

Washington DC is the US capital city. Puerto Rico is a US commonwealth. This means it is governed by its own people.

6

REGIONS OF THE UNITED STATES

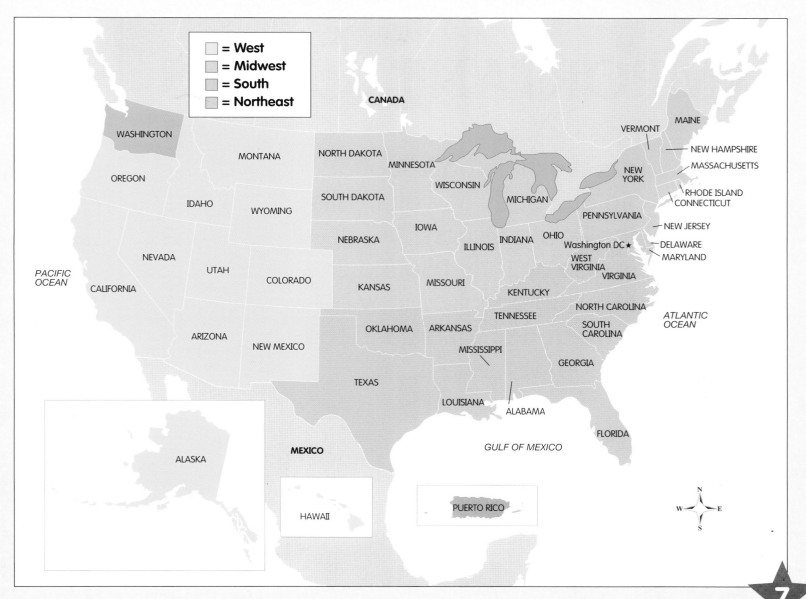

= West
= Midwest
= South
= Northeast

CANADA

WASHINGTON

MONTANA

NORTH DAKOTA

MINNESOTA

VERMONT

MAINE

NEW HAMPSHIRE

OREGON

IDAHO

WYOMING

SOUTH DAKOTA

WISCONSIN

MICHIGAN

NEW YORK

MASSACHUSETTS

RHODE ISLAND
CONNECTICUT

PENNSYLVANIA

NEVADA

UTAH

COLORADO

NEBRASKA

IOWA

ILLINOIS

INDIANA

OHIO

Washington DC ★

NEW JERSEY

DELAWARE

MARYLAND

PACIFIC
OCEAN

CALIFORNIA

KANSAS

MISSOURI

WEST
VIRGINIA

VIRGINIA

KENTUCKY

ARIZONA

NEW MEXICO

OKLAHOMA

ARKANSAS

TENNESSEE

NORTH CAROLINA

SOUTH
CAROLINA

ATLANTIC
OCEAN

TEXAS

MISSISSIPPI

GEORGIA

LOUISIANA

ALABAMA

FLORIDA

GULF OF MEXICO

ALASKA

MEXICO

HAWAII

PUERTO RICO

N
W   E
S

7

IMPORTANT CITIES

Olympia is Washington's **capital**. It is located on the southern tip of a body of water called Puget Sound. This is part of the Pacific Ocean.

Seattle is also on Puget Sound. It is the state's largest city, with 608,660 people. Many businesses are based in Seattle's **metropolitan** area. Goods pass through the city's roads and waterways.

8

Washington

Seattle
Tacoma
Olympia
Spokane

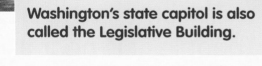

Washington's state capitol is also called the Legislative Building.

People often travel by large ferryboats in the Seattle area.

Spokane (spoh-KAN) is Washington's second-largest city. It is home to 208,916 people. It is located on the Spokane River near Idaho's border.

Tacoma is the state's third-largest city, with 198,397 people. It is near the Olympic and Cascade Mountains. And, the Puyallup River flows through the city.

Spokane has waterfalls that provide power for the city.

Tacoma is located on Commencement Bay, which is part of Puget Sound.

11

WASHINGTON IN HISTORY

Washington's history includes Native Americans, explorers, and settlers. Native Americans have lived in present-day Washington for thousands of years. Spanish explorers visited the land in 1775.

People continued to explore the area. They discovered its rich **resources**, such as animal furs, forests, and water. Gold was found in the area in the mid-1800s. This brought many settlers to the Washington Territory in the 1860s. In 1889, Washington became a state.

After gold was found, towns such as Walla Walla grew. Settlers arrived and started businesses there.

Timeline

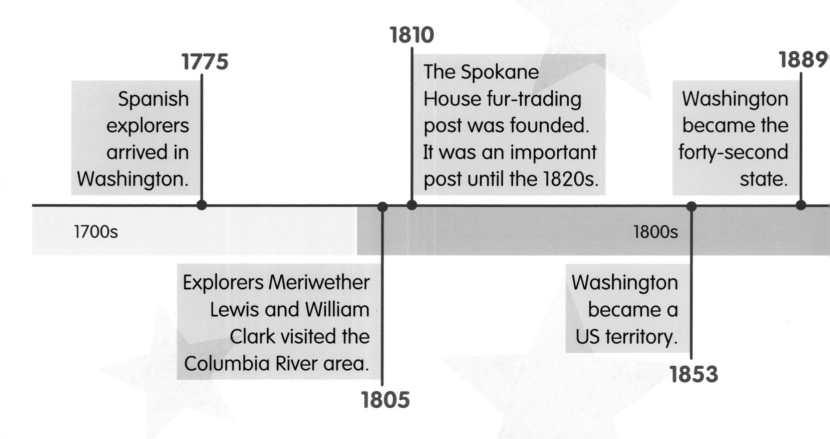

1810

1775

Spanish explorers arrived in Washington.

The Spokane House fur-trading post was founded. It was an important post until the 1820s.

1889

Washington became the forty-second state.

1700s

1800s

Explorers Meriwether Lewis and William Clark visited the Columbia River area.

Washington became a US territory.

1805

1853

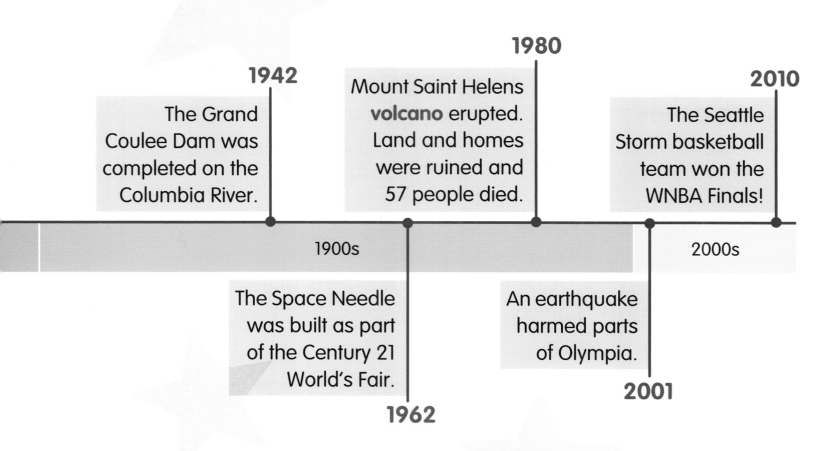

1942

The Grand Coulee Dam was completed on the Columbia River.

1980

Mount Saint Helens **volcano** erupted. Land and homes were ruined and 57 people died.

2010

The Seattle Storm basketball team won the WNBA Finals!

1900s

2000s

The Space Needle was built as part of the Century 21 World's Fair.

1962

An earthquake harmed parts of Olympia.

2001

15

ACROSS THE LAND

Washington has mountains, valleys, **volcanoes**, forests, lakes, and rivers. It is on the Pacific Ocean. Puget Sound and the Columbia River are important waterways. The Olympic and Cascade mountain ranges cover parts of the state.

Many types of animals make their homes in Washington. These include bears, deer, ducks, geese, and trout.

Did You Know?

In July, the average temperature in Washington is 66°F (19°C). In January, it is 30°F (-1°C).

Washington has thick forests filled with evergreen trees. That's why it is called "the Evergreen State."

EARNING A LIVING

Washington has many important businesses. Most people work in service jobs, such as shipping goods or helping visitors to the state. Others work for companies that make computers and airplane parts.

Washington has many natural **resources**. Fish and shellfish are caught in the coastal waters. Apples, mint, potatoes, and greenhouse plants are grown in the state. Dairy products and beef cattle also come from Washington's farms.

Timber is an important product from Washington.

Natural Wonder

The Olympic Mountains are in northwest Washington. They cover about 3,500 square miles (9,000 sq km) of land. Large, old trees grow in mossy forests there. And, the mountains are known for having **glaciers** and waterfalls.

Olympic National Park covers much of the Olympic Mountains. People visit the park to hike, camp, and fish.

Did You Know?

Washington is known for rain. Some parts of the Olympic Mountains get more than 140 inches (356 cm) of rain each year. This is one of the highest rainfall amounts in the United States.

The Hoh Rainforest is in Olympic National Park.

HOMETOWN HEROES

Many famous people are from Washington. Bing Crosby was born in Tacoma in 1903. He was a singer and actor. He started out in the 1920s.

By the 1940s, Crosby was known for acting in movies. He acted in more than 60 movies, including *Holiday Inn* in 1942. In this movie, he sang the famous song "White Christmas."

Crosby's given name was Harry Lillis Crosby.

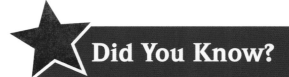

Did You Know?

Gates was in high school when he started his first computer software company!

Bill Gates was born in Seattle in 1955. He is famous for his work with personal computers.

In 1975, he cofounded Microsoft Corporation. Today, Microsoft makes **software** and other computer products. Gates is known for his ideas and wealth. He is also known for his **charity** work.

In 1994, Gates and his wife started a charity that helps people around the world.

Tour Book

Do you want to go to Washington? If you visit the state, here are some places to go and things to do!

 ## Cheer

Take in a Seattle Mariners game! This baseball team plays at Safeco Field.

 ## Play

Touch snow in July at Mount Rainier National Park! People hike and drive through this park to see its forests and glaciers.

 Discover

Visit Mount Saint Helens National Volcanic Monument. Learn about the volcano's major eruption in 1980. Its most recent activity ended in 2008.

View

Ride to the top of Seattle's famous Space Needle! It is 605 feet (184 m) tall. You can see for many miles from its observation deck.

See

Twilight book fans can visit the real-life town of Forks! It is located near the Olympic Mountains northwest of Seattle.

A GREAT STATE

The story of Washington is important to the United States. The people and places that make up this state offer something special to the country. Together with all the states, Washington helps make the United States great.

Palouse Falls State Park is in southeastern Washington.
The falls drop down about 200 feet (60 m)!

29

Fast Facts

Date of Statehood:
November 11, 1889

Population (rank):
6,724,540
(13th most-populated state)

Total Area (rank):
68,095 square miles
(21st largest state)

Motto:
"Alki"
(By and By)

Nickname:
Evergreen State,
Chinook State

State Capital:
Olympia

Flag:

Flower: Coast Rhododendron

Postal Abbreviation:
WA

Tree: Western Hemlock

Bird: Willow Goldfinch

Important Words

capital a city where government leaders meet.

charity a group or a fund that helps people in need.

diverse made up of things that are different from each other.

glacier (GLAY-shuhr) a huge chunk of ice and snow on land.

metropolitan of or relating to a large city, usually with nearby smaller cities called suburbs.

region a large part of a country that is different from other parts.

resource a supply of something useful or valued.

software the programs that make a computer operate.

volcano a deep vent, or opening, in Earth's surface from which hot liquid rock or steam comes out.

Web Sites

To learn more about Washington, visit ABDO Publishing Company online. Web sites about Washington are featured on our Book Links page. These links are routinely monitored and updated to provide the most current information available.

www.abdopublishing.com

Index